101 Cooles
Do in

Introduction

So you're going to Cuba, huh? You lucky lucky thing! You are sure in for a treat because Cuba is truly one of the most magical and unexplored countries on this planet.

In Havana, you'll find incredible colonial architecture and a party scene that cannot be matched, whilst further afield, you can find some of the very best beaches of the Caribbean, and natural parks that offer up incredible opportunities for hiking, climbing, and cycling.

In this guide, we'll be giving you the low down on:
- the very best things to shove in your pie hole, from street food on the streets of Havana to fancy seafood restaurants
- the best shopping so that you can take a little piece of Cuba back home with you, whether that's in the form of the best cigar you've ever tried, or a bottle of delicious Cuban rum

- incredible festivals, whether you would like to rock out to Cuban bands in the countryside or you'd prefer a little more sophistication with the Havana Ballet Festival

- the coolest historical and cultural sights that you simply cannot afford to miss from ancient burial sites to incredible fortresses

- the best places to have a few mojitos and party with the local people

- and tonnes more coolness besides!

Let's not waste any more time – here are the 101 coolest things not to miss in Cuba!

1. Discover Cuban History in a Grand Palace

If you want to have a real understanding of Cuba, it's imperative that you have an understanding of the Cuban Revolution, which took place during the 1950s. The best place to learn about this important time in the country's history is at the Museum of the Revolution in Havana. As well as having the chance to look at some incredible memorabilia from this time, the museum is also housed within the former presidential palace, and it's extraordinarily beautiful.

(Avenida Bélgica, La Habana)

2. Cool Down With a Blended Batido

When your budget can't quite stretch to the fourth daiquiri of the day, but you are in desperate need of a frozen treat to cool you down, fear not, because if you head out on to the streets you'll be able to find plenty of batidos, and these are essentially the Cuban version of a smoothie. You can get them in all different kinds of flavours such as coconut, and lime, but our favourite has to be the sweet guava flavour. Super refreshing.

3. Take in a Show at the Gran Teatro de la Habana

If you are looking for a reason to get dressed up and enjoy an unforgettable night out in Havana, you absolutely need to know about the Gran Teatro de la Habana, one of the most important theatres in the capital city. The theatre is located in the Galician district of the city, and was originally constructed, in the early 20th century, to act as a social hub for the Galician community. These days, it's one of the best places in Havana to take in a ballet show, and the Cuban National Ballet often performs there.

(458 Paseo de Martí, La Habana;

www.balletcuba.cult.cu/gran-teatro-de-la-habana)

4. Snorkel in the Sea of Varadero

If what you are looking for on your trip to Cuba is beach, you cannot do any better than the gorgeous coastal town of Varadero. This is actually the largest beach resort in all of the Caribbean, making it the ideal place for sun, sand, and endless beach activities. If the

days of lying on the beach become tiresome, the good
news is that the water is super clear and really ideal for
snorkelling and diving expeditions so you can explore
the coral and tropical fish beneath the sea.

5. Hang Out in Hemingway's Favourite Bar, Floridita

One of the most famous residents of Havana is
certainly Ernest Hemingway, and many people like to
retrace the famous writer's steps while they are in the
city. One of his favourite hangouts was a fish restaurant
and cocktail bar that goes by the name of Floridita and
it is still operational today. In fact, this place opened
200 years ago and is still popular as it ever was. The
daiquiri, a drink that was invented in Cuba, is
particularly good in this bar.

(Obispo, La Habana; www.floridita-cuba.com)

6. Go Birdwatching in Parque Nacional Cienaga de Zapata

Cuba is a country with extremely diverse wildlife, and it's difficult not to be bowled away by all the animals you can see in the various national parks around the country. If you are particularly into birdwatching, the Parque Nacional Cienaga de Zapata is 100% the place for you. Bring along your binoculars and you will be able to spot Cuban Crows, Cuban Parrots, Cuban Peewees, Cuban Pygmy Owls, and many other species besides.

7. Visit the Most Stunning Cemetery You Will Ever See

In the Western world, cemeteries are more often than not an incredibly sombre affair, but that is not the case in Latin America, and certainly not in Cuba where you can find one of the most grandiose and spectacular cemeteries that exists anywhere in the world, the Necropolis Cristobal Colon. Inside this graveyard you'll find incredible religious iconography and lots of colour. It's a good idea to purchase the walking guide from the entrance so you can also discover the tombstones of many famous Cubans as you stroll around.

8. Cool Off in the Caburni Waterfall

While Trinidad is an exceptionally beautiful town, if you find yourself in the town with a longing to escape the streets for some nature, you're in luck because the Salto de Caburni waterfall is just around the corner. In fact, you can take a brisk 7km hike in one of Cuba's natural parks, through dense forests and rocky outcroppings to reach this beautiful waterfall. Getting there early is a very good idea, because the natural swimming pool at the bottom of the falls can fill up in the afternoon.

9. Stroll Through the Rooms of Capitolio Nacional

A city full of grandiose and spectacular buildings, the Capitolio Nacional in Cuba might just be the most impressive of them all. The building was designed and built following the country's sugar boom, and it cost a staggering $17 million to build. Actually, this isn't hard to believe if you take the opportunity to stroll around the building yourself. The whole building was constructed with limestone and granite, giving it a feeling of incredible opulence, and there are many statues and grand artwork throughout the building.

(422 Industria, La Habana)

10. Enjoy an Evening of Rum Tasting at Casa Del Ron

Of course, one of the most famous products that comes from Cuba is rum, and what better way to get acquainted with this delicious tipple than to spend an enjoyable evening sipping on the good stuff? Well, that is exactly what you are invited to do at Casa Del Ron in trendy Varadero. The old building of the Casa is nothing short of stunning, and the selection of rum on the premises is equally impressive. The friendly staff would be more than happy to take you through a guided tasting.

(Avenida 1ra, Varadero)

11. Learn More About Hemingway's Life in Cuba

Perhaps the most famous expat to have ever lived in Cuba is the writer Ernest Hemingway. During the 1940s, the novelist bought a villa on a hill that lies 15km southeast of the city, and he lived there up until 1960. The inside of the museum has remained completely unchanged since the day the writer left, and the estate has been converted into a museum dedicated to the man, his works, and his life in Cuba. It is quite astounding to see the man's very own book, record, and antiques collection up close in the place where he actually lived and worked.

(Singer, La Habana; www.hemingwaycuba.com/finca-la-vigia.html)

12. Hit a Few Balls at Varadero Golf Club

If your idea of a perfect getaway is to take to the golf club and hit a few balls, the place that you need to head straight for in Varadero, which is more of a resort town, and is equipped with things like state of the art golf courses. The Varadero Golf Club was the very first

18 hole golf course to be designed in Cuba. Just don't blame us if the glorious sight of the ocean on the horizon distracts you from your game.

(Autopista Sur, Varadero; www.varaderogolfclub.com)

13. Visit One of the Strangest Chinatowns in the World

The idea of Chinatown is something that exists right throughout the world, and you can find Chinatowns in places like London, Mexico City and Tokyo. But perhaps one of the most bizarre Chinatowns of them all exists in Havana. Back in the mid 19th century, Cuba actually had one of the largest Chinese populations in all of Latin America, but these days the place is just a little bit strange because there are hardly any Chinese people there. Still, if you fancy a break from the regular beans and rice of Cuba, it's worth a visit.

14. Go Horseback Riding Through the Tobacco Fields of Vinales

The Vinales Valley is one of the best loved places of natural beauty in all of Cuba, and while you can hike or cycle across these landscapes, it can be a great idea to have a real adventure and explore the authentic way on horseback. This is the tobacco soul of western Cuba, and as you ride along, you will be able to see the lush tobacco fields, and you'll also see the farmers doing their day-to-day work in the fields. You might even see coffee plantations and caves on your visit.

15. Visit a Cigar Factory in Baracoa

Cuba is world famous for the incredible quality of its cigars, and while it can be great to puff on a few and even take some home as gifts, it's even better to really get under the skin of cigar culture in Cuba by visiting a cigar factory. While visitors are very welcome, this cigar factory actually isn't really on the tourist path and doesn't attract many people through its doors, so you might just have the experience all to yourself.

16. Take a Steam Train to the Valley of the Sugar Mills

Of course, one of the most famous things about Cuba is its sugar mills, and a trip to this Latin island would not be complete without learning more about this aspect of the country's culture. There is no more beautiful way of doing this than by taking a steam train into the valley of the sugar mills. You will see the sugar fields where the slaves used to sadly toil away, and walk through the architecture of the sugar barons of Cuba.

17. Chill Out in Arty Tapas Bar, Espacios

When it gets to the evening time in Havana and you are stuck for something to do, we can highly recommend a trip to one of the city's best tapas bars, Espacios. Havana really doesn't have much of a hipster scene, but if hipsters did exist in Havana, you can bet your bottom dollar that they would congregate here at Espacios, where there is a lovely cocktail menu, yummy tapas, and an outdoor terrace where you'll feel perfectly relaxed.

(Calle 10, La Habana; http://espacios-habana.com)

18. Say Hi to the Pink Flamingos at Caya Coco

With its tropical climate, Cuba is a country that attracts some beautiful wildlife. If you want to discover some of the country's incredible animal life for yourself, we highly recommend a trip to Caya Coco, which is a gorgeous beach on the north coast of Cuba. As if the snowy white sands aren't impressive enough, when you arrive, you are likely to see the pink flamingo colonies that call this beach home, as well as many other beautiful bird species.

19. Buy Some Beautiful Pottery at Taller de Ceramica Artistica

While Cuba doesn't have the handicrafts culture of many other Latin American cultures, there are still some pockets of handicrafts in the country, and these are well worth exploring if you would like to take back something really special from Cuba with you. The Taller de Ceramica Artistica in Varadero might just be the #1 place for ceramics in all of Cuba. Everything is

made on the premises, and you can even have
something custom made for you.

20. Visit the Oldest House in Cuba, Casa de Diego Velazquez

If you really want to get to grips with the history of
Cuba, you simply have to visit the oldest house in the
country, Casa de Diego Velazquez. This house was
built in 1522 and was the house of the island's very first
governor. Today, you can walk around the house and
check out a display of 16th to 19th century furnishings
and artworks, but simply being in the house transports
you to a world of Cuba from centuries ago.
(Francisco Vicente Aguilera, Santiago de Cuba)

21. Have an Artsy Evening at Fabrica de Arte Cubano

The Fabrica de Arte Cubano is, without a doubt, one
of the most important cultural spaces in Havana, and
actually in the whole country. This place is the
brainchild of the Afro-Cuban musician X-Alfonso, and

it's a place where all of the arts intersect. One day you might see a fashion show, the next day a piece of experimental dance, and in the café you can always find people hotly debating the arts culture of Cuba. If you want a cultural evening in the city, be sure to keep up to date with their programme.

(Calle 26, La Habana)

22. Indulge a Sweet Tooth With Streetside Churros

If you stick to the tourist currency, eating your meals out in Havana can be more than a little bit pricey, but if you keep your eyes open and you're a little bit canny, you can enjoy delicious food on the street and pay a fraction of the price with local Cuban pesos. If you can't complete a meal without something sweet, you'll be pleased to know that you can find churros vendors all over Old Havana. You'll spot the best vendors from the long lines on the streets!

23. Dance in the Open Air in Trinidad's Music Alley

As well as being beautiful and rich in history, Cuba is simply really really fun. There is music and dancing at all hours of the day, and you can find some of that Cuban spirit for yourself at the Palenque de Los Congos Reales in Trinidad, which is otherwise known as the Music Alley. On this open patio, you can find every kind of music under the sun. You can dance to salsa, poetic trova songs, but our favourite is the rumba music, paired with frenetic dancing, and sometimes fire eating.

24. Watch the Boat Races of the Varadero Regatta

If you want to get a little taste of how the upper classes live in Cuba, there is nothing quite like visiting a formal regatta at a port town. Regattas are more commonly associated with places like Cannes and Monaco, but we reckon that the Varadero Regatta can give them a run for their money. This historic regatta dates way back to 1910, and you can experience a variety of boat races, as well as epic parties in the town when it takes place every May.

25. Hike to the Top of Pico Turquino

Pico Turquino is the highest point in all of Cuba, and, of course, that makes it a must visit destination for all intrepid adventurers who love to scale mountains. This peak is pretty remote, located in the southeast part of the country where many tourists don't venture, and so it can make for a really incredible exploration. It is a good idea to start a hike from Las Cuevas, and if you are not so experienced, there are many tour companies that can help you on your way.

26. Enjoy a Night of Cabaret at Cabaret Parisien

For a night of entertainment in Cuba's capital city, you needn't look any further than the Cabaret Parisien, which is hosted nightly at the Hotel Nacional. As you can probably tell from the name, this is a take on a French cabaret show, but there is a strong injection of

Latin spirit into the whole thing. The costumes are nothing short of spectacular, the performers are all extremely accomplished dancers, and at the end of the night you are invited to the dancefloor as show transforms into a disco.

27. Try Deep Sea Fishing at Marina Gaviota

If you love nothing more than an afternoon of relaxing fishing, you might want to elevate your fishing game on your trip to Cuba, with a deep sea fishing expedition at Marina Gaviota. There are a few tour companies who will take you on Hemingway's fishing trail for an afternoon, including food and drink and board. But the real highlight is the fishing, and you'll have the opportunity to fish for barracudas, tuna, red snapper, king mackerel, blue marlin, and more.

28. Learn All About Rum in Santiago de Cuba

If you are going to drink one tipple during your time in Cuba, it simply has to be rum. And what better way to learn about rum than visiting a museum dedicated to the good stuff? That's exactly what you can do at the Museo de Ron in Santiago de Cuba. The friendly staff will guide you through this old townhouse and show you the old ways that rum was produced right up to the present day. And there is a bar on site so you can enjoy a cocktail while you learn.

29. Brush Up Your Spanish Skills

Spanish is, of course, the national language of Cuba. And brushing up on your Spanish skills while in Cuba can be a great idea, because the Cuban accent is very thick, and because you'll find many people who don't speak a word of English. If you have the time, it can be a great idea to spend your first week within one of the many Spanish schools in Cuba. We are particularly fond of StudyTeam Cuba, which is located in Trinidad, and all the classes take place in the homes of local people.

(www.studyteam.com)

30. Enjoy Lazy Beach Days at Jibacoa

When you visit Cuba for a beach getaway, the most obvious place to go is Varadero. And while the beaches here are totally stunning, the resort heavy area doesn't really give you a sense of the "real" Cuba. If you want to take a beach vacation where the Cuban locals go, you'd be much better off discovering the charming fishing town of Jibacoa. The vibe here is much more rustic, and you will have the opportunity to see how an working fishing town lives today.

31. Take in a Show at the Teatro Nacional de Cuba

For an evening of unforgettable entertainment, you need to know about the Teatro Nacional de Cuba, or National Theatre of Cuba, located in Havana. This theatre was constructed during the years of the Cuban Revolution, and these days you can catch all kinds of great performances inside the theatre. On the main stage, you can find performances such as epic ballet shows and Shakespeare plays, and there are also smaller stages where you can catch more experimental performances.

32. Visit a Microbrewery in Havana

When you think of drinking in Cuba, you will probably think of rum, mojitos, and daiquiris first of all. And while these are great, sometimes all you want is a chilled beer. Well, fear not, because Havana also has its very own microbrewery called La Factoria Plaza Vieja, which you are very welcome to visit. The freshly made beer tastes great on a hot day in Cuba, and there is also barbecued chicken available, which makes it go down even better.

(San Ignacio, La Habana)

33. Join in With the Carnaval Festivities in Santiago de Cuba

Carnaval is something celebrated all over the world in Catholic countries, and Cuba is no different. But while Carnaval usually takes place in February, in Santiago de Cuba, the Carnaval celebrations are slightly different, and they take place at the end of July each year. The celebrations last for two weeks and everything on the streets is pure joy during that time. You'll see incredible drumming, spectacular costumes, fire juggling, eating and drinking on the street, and wonderful dancing. Why not join in with the fun?

34. Take in an Event at Casa de Las Americas

Founded just months following the Cuba Revolution, Casa de las Americas was created in Havana with the purpose of extending socio-cultural relations to other countries in Latin America and the Caribbean. It is now the best-known and most prestigious cultural institution in all of Cuba. On any given day, you can catch an exciting event at Casa de Las Americas, whether it's an art exhibition, a literary debate, a poetry reading, or a contemporary dance performance.
(www.casa.co.cu)

35. Visit the Studio of Cuban Artist, Jose Fuster

To get to grips with the real Havana, you have to veer away from the centre of the city, and head into the suburbs. Head west into the suburbs of Jaimanitas and you will find something extra special, particularly for arts lovers. This is where the local Cuban artist, Jose Fuster, is attempting to transform his neighbourhood into a public work of art. The centre of this experiment is his open studio where you can see many of his paintings and sculptures, and if you are lucky, you might even see the man at work himself.

(Calle 226, Havana)

36. Discover the Real Cuba in Beautiful Remedios

If you want to get off the beaten path and to discover the "real" Cuba, just as it was one hundred years ago, we can't recommend the town of Remedios strongly enough. Although this is Cuba's second oldest settlement, dating back to the early 16th century, it is rarely visited by tourists. There is beautiful colonial architecture, lots of stalls selling street food, a slow way of life, and a hell of a lot of charm.

37. Shop For Souvenirs at Havana's Open-Air Handicrafts Market

Before leaving Cuba, you will no doubt want to take back some souvenirs so that you can always remember this extraordinarily special part of the world. And the best place for a spot of shopping is at the open air market in Havana called Almacenes San Jose. While it's true that Cuba doesn't have the handicrafts culture of other Latin American countries, it has grown a lot over the last three decades, and in the market you'll find belts, shoes, bags, ceramics, posters, and much more besides.

(Avenida del Puerto corner of Calle Cuba, Havana)

38. Get Artsy at the Havana Art Biennial

If you are an arts lover, there is one event on the Cuban calendar that you should know about above all others, the Havana Art Biennial. This annual event was created in 1984 and is still going strong today, with many artists from around the world being invited to showcase the works at the biennial, which takes place each year in November. If you are looking for an original piece of artwork to take home with you, this would be the perfect place to make a purchase. *(www.biennialfoundation.org/ biennials/ havana-biennale)*

39. Visit a Horse Cart Production Line

Okay, we recognise that it probably isn't your priority to learn about horse carts on your trip to Cuba, but if you have a spare morning, this is a delightful way to pass a few hours. In the charming city of Bayamo, you can find the only handcrafted horse cart production line in the whole country, Fabrica de los Coches. You are welcome to chat to the makers, who take roughly three months to make every wooden cart by hand. And while it's not possible to take one home with you, you can purchase them in miniature models.

40. Shop for Cigars at La Casa del Habano

Of course, Cuba is more than just a little bit famous for the quality of its cigars, but if you are a first timer to the country, it can be difficult to know where to go to get your hands on the real deal. Without a doubt, the cigar shop with the best reputation is La Casa del Habano. The staff are extremely knowledgeable and can select the very best cigar for you, and there is even a cigar lounge inside where you can puff away.

(CD, La Habana)

41. Take it All Off at Cayo Largo

While Cuba is certainly a conservative country, this doesn't mean that there are not pockets of more progressive attitudes in the country, and nowhere is this more evident than at the beautiful Cayo Largo beach, where you might get more than you bargain for as you stroll along the white sands. Why so? Well, Cayo Largo is the only beach in Cuba where nudism is commonplace, so if you feel like getting an all over tan, this is the place for you.

42. Enjoy a Luxurious Stay at Villa DuPont

If your idea of a perfect vacation is to immerse yourself in luxury during every minute of your trip, you absolutely need to know about the Villa DuPont in

Cuba, one of the most renowned and celebrated hotels in the country. Otherwise known as Xanadu Mansion, there are only 6 colonial style rooms, so this place is extremely exclusive, and every room is filled with antique furniture. Staying here also gives you access to the Varadero Golf Club.

(Dupont De Nemours,carretera Las Americas Km 8 1/2,autopista Sur Varadero)

43. See How Cuban Cowboys Party at Jornada Cucalambeana

When you think of the music culture of Cuba, you probably think of frenetic salsa or rumba sounds, and while that is certainly part of the national identity, the local people also have a passion for Cuban country music. Jornada Cucalambeana is the biggest annual celebration of this type of music, when Cuban cowboys recite their 10 line verses to music, in the hopes of entertaining the local crowd. The festival takes place in June just outside Las Tunas.

44. Go Freshwater Fishing in Cienfuegos

If your idea of the perfect relaxing vacation is to put a fishing rod into the waters of the lake while waiting for a bite and watching the world go by, you are in luck because there are numerous fishing opportunities in Cuba. One of the best places is around Cienfugeos. On the edge of this city, you can find Embalse Hanabanilla, which is a reservoir with 36 square kilometres of space. It has the largest collection of largemouth bass in the world, so it's a great place to get a catch.

45. Have an Adventure in the Gran Caverna de Santo Tomas

If your idea of a good time away is not walking from one stuffy museum to another but actually getting out there and exploring the wild landscapes of a country, Cuba has a lot to offer, and specifically with the Gran Caverna de Santo Tomas, which is the largest cave system in Cuba, and the second largest in the Americas. It is possible to take a 90 minute tour through a part of the caves, which includes bats, stalactites, stalagmites, underground pools, incredible rock formations, and bats.

46. Enjoy the El Reve Changui Festival in Baracoa

Cubans certainly do love to have a good time, and so it can be a fantastic idea to time your Cuba trip so that it coincides with one of the many exciting festivals that takes place on the island during the year. One of our favourites is the El Reve Changui Festival, which is hosted in Baracoa every December around Christmas time. The best Changui artists from around Cuba are invited to participate, and there is always plenty of music and dancing on the streets.

47. Immerse Yourself in Nature in a Gigantic Orchid Garden

Cuba isn't all cigars and mojitos. There is also plenty of natural beauty to explore within the country, and truthfully, it doesn't get much more beautiful than the Orquideario Soroa, which lies about 95km southwest of the capital city. Inside this stunning garden, you can find a collection of over 700 types of orchid, the largest collection in all of Cuba, with many species that are native to the country.

48. Have a Zip Lining Adventure Over the Loma de Fortin Canopy

If you fancy yourself as something of an adventurer, there are plenty of adventures to be had while you are in Cuba, and many of these adventures can be found in the spectacular Vinales Valley. If you've done the hiking and the horseback riding, and you are still longing for more adventure, the zip line that extends right over the Loma de Fortin Canopy can be a great idea. The zip line is connected across eight elevated platforms, so you get to experience huge amounts of the wilderness at a great height.

49. Dance to Frenetic Rumba Music at Callejon de Hamel

If you love nothing more than to shake what God gave you of an evening time, you are in luck, because Cubans certainly do love to dance, and they dance very well. One of our favourite places for a shimmy in Havana is at the Callejon de Hamel, a funky place that attracts a fun loving crowd who love to dance to frenetic rumba tunes all through the night. It's only open on a Sunday, so make sure that you have this one firmly etched into your itinerary.

50. Hike the El Yunque Mountain in Baracoa

El Yunque mountain is a particularly special place in Cuba because it was mentioned by Christopher Columbus on his explorations of the Americas. This mountain is around 575 metres high, and has a flat top that makes it look like an anvil. If you are an adventurer, a hike up this mountain could be the highlight of your trip to Cuba. It's both hot and muddy, but there are many tour companies that can help you to scale this mountain.

51. Go Gourmet at the Varadero Gourmet Festival

Let's face it, Cuba is not a country that is famed for its incredible cuisine. Rice and beans is normally order of the day, but if you fancy treating yourself to something a little fancier, then you should coincide your Cuba trip with the Varadero Gourmet Festival, which is hosted at the end of June each year. Top chefs are invited to demonstrate how Cuban cooking can be elevated to the next level, and there's always plenty of tastings so you can chow down on all the deliciousness.

52. Watch a Baseball Game at Estadio Manuel Fuentes Borges

If you are a sporty kind of person, you might to want to take in a live baseball match while you're in Cuba, as this is a sport that the locals are crazy about. While the biggest baseball stadium is in the capital city, we think that the Estadio Manuel Fuentes Borges in Baracoa is much more charming. The really lovely thing about this small stadium is that it sits right on the beach, which is something very unique for a baseball court.

53. Discover the Sweet Treat of Baracoa, Cucurucho

While in Baracoa, there is little more pleasurable than walking the streets and munching on some freshly made cucurucho, which is a street dessert native to this small city. Essentially, a cone shaped palm leaf is filled with coconut sugar, and other flavours such as orange, guava, and pineapple. This is very much a street snack, which means that you can pay in the local currency and save your pennies.

54. Learn How to Dance Like a Real Cuban

As you head to the bars and clubs of Cuba in the evening time, one thing that you are sure to notice is just how well the local Cubans can move their hips in time to music, while making it seem perfectly effortless. If you want to learn how to dance just like a real Cuban on your trip, why not take some dance lessons? We think that Trinidad is the perfect city for this and the Casa de la Cultura skill is the perfect place, as it can cater to total beginners. Now you really have no excuse.

55. Chow Down on Seafood Risotto at Café Laurent

We're gonna be straight with you – Cuban food can be hit and miss. The traditional food is very beans and rice oriented, and often doesn't use herbs and spices. But if you want to treat yourself, there are a handful of restaurants that are worth visiting for a more interesting culinary experience. Café Laurent in Havana is one of our favourites. This place has a Spanish Basque based menu that consists of shrimps, steaks, seafood, and salads, and our favourite thing has to be the yummy seafood risotto.

(Penthouse, 257 Calle M, La Habana)

56. Find Something Special at the Havana International Crafts Fair

On your last days in Cuba, you'll no doubt be scrambling for souvenirs to take home. But with a little forward planning, you can coincide a trip with the Havana International Crafts Fair so that you can take back something really special with you. This fair usually takes place at the beginning of December, and around 400 craftspeople have stalls. This means that whether you want jewellery, candles, original artwork, or ceramics, there will be something special for you.

57. Take a Selfie With Cuba's Oldest Cactus, El Patriarca

Cuba might be a little bit behind the times when it comes to technology (best of luck finding wifi!), but that doesn't mean that you can't inject a little 21st century life into the country by taking selfies, and one of the best spots for a selfie snap is with El Patriarca, the oldest cactus in the country. This is a giant treelike cactus that stands tall with a height of more than twenty feet, and it is presumed to be around 600 years old.

58. Discover Beautiful Objects in the Museo Romantico

You don't have to be a die hard romantic to enjoy a trip to the Museo Romantico., because the name actually refers to the Romantic period of Cuban history in the mid 19th century. This museum in the city of Trinidad will give any visitor a fantastic glimpse into the life of wealthy sugar barons in that period as this gorgeous mansion was owned by a sugar baron who went by the name of Conde de Brunet. Inside you'll find antique furniture, beautiful ceramics, and lavish artworks.

(52 Calle Cristo, Trinidad)

59. Cycle to the Beautiful White Sands of Ancon Beach

If you are a beach bum, you'll have no problem finding some beautiful white sands in Cuba, and probably the best beach on the south coast is Playa Ancon. The beach lies 12km south of Trinidad, and it can be very nice to cycle from the town to the beach. Once at Playa Ancon, you will find 4 kilometres of white sand, and the most beautiful seas in varying shades of stunning blue. Perfect for when you need to recharge your batteries.

60. Catch Some Awesome Shows at the Havana Theatre Festival

If you are an arts lover, it's a brilliant idea to coincide your trip to Cuba with the Havana Theatre Festival, which is hosted in the capital city around the end of October. You don't need to worry if your Spanish isn't up to scratch because this is actually an international theatre festival with performers invited from all around the world. Each year, there are more than 70 shows, so whether you want some contemporary drama or a circus show, there will be something for you.

61. Sip on Fresh Sugar Cane Juice

There are two things that Cuba is famous for. Its blisteringly warm weather, and its part in the sugar industry. Well, put the two together and you have something really magical, because sipping on juice fresh from the sugar cane on a hot day is a pleasure unlike any other. On the streets of Havana and many other places within Cuba, you can find men and women on the street, grinding the sugar cane through a machine to release the fresh natural juices.

62. Learn All About Napoleon Bonaparte

Napoleon Bonaparte is one of the most important figures in European military history, and so you might not expect to find a museum dedicated to the man in Cuba, but indeed you can, and it's also a pretty incredible museum. At the Museo Napoleonico in Havana, you have the chance to peruse 8000 objects that the man himself used during different phases of his life. You'll be able to see guns he carried at the battle of Borodino, a telescope of his, and tonnes more fascinating objects besides. *(San Miguel 1159, Havana)*

63. Explore a Stunning Fort in Santiago de Cuba

While Cuba might be more famous for its rum and dancing than its historic attractions, if you are a history buff, you certainly won't be disappointed on a trip to Cuba. Castillo de San Pedro is a stunning fort in Santiago de Cuba that you simply shouldn't miss. Construction started in 1637 as a way to safeguard against raiding pirates, and indeed, those ideas were well founded because the fortress protected the city on numerus occasions. It is now a UNESCO Heritage Site.

64. Enjoy a Cuban Barbecue at La Fontana

When you have consumed just about as much beans and rice as you can possibly handle, treat yourself to a meat feast at La Fontana in Havana, which specialises in Cuban barbecue. The really nice thing about this place is that they don't just serve up any grilled meats, but use a full on charcoal grill that imparts an incredibly smoky taste. And if you fancy something a little lighter, the lobster ceviche and the beef carpaccio are also super delicious.

(www.lafontanahavana.com)

65. Enjoy Las Vegas Style Nightlife at Tropicana Nightclub

Havana is the ultimate city for dancing all night long and watching spectacular shows. No doubt the most popular show and club night in the city of Havana is the Tropicana Club. Quite unbelievably, this club has been entertaining the masses in Cuba since 1939, and these days you can still expect the most lavish costumes, spectacular dance routines, and pumping live music. Why not join in with the fun?

(72 A, La Habana; www.cabaret-tropicana.com)

66. Take a Horse Ride to Maguana Beach

There are plenty of beaches to enjoy in Cuba, but if you want to get to the off the beaten track hidden gems, we can totally recommend a day trip to charming Maguana beach, which lies just around 20km north of Baracoa. The whole setup is totally rustic with simple seafood shacks on the beach and unspoiled sand. If you really want to be taken back in time, it can also be a great idea to take a horse ride along the sands.

67. Go Chocolate Crazy in Baracoa

If you are a chocolate fan, and who isn't, Baracoa needs to be your destination of choice. In fact, as soon as you are in the city, you will smell the chocolate all over the streets. And the epicentre for chocolate in the city has to be Casa Del Cacao, a café meets museum that tells the history of cacao in the eastern region of Cuba. Best of all, they serve up thick and rich cups of hot chocolate, and they also sell their own delightfully bitter chocolate bars.

(Maravi, Baracoa)

68. Enjoy an Afternoon Coffee at Plaza Vieja

Of course, there is plenty to see and do in Havana, but sometimes all you want to do is have a smooth cup of a coffee while taking in a nice view, right? If that sounds like a morning well spent to you, you should absolutely know about the Plaza Vieja, one of the most important and popular plazas located in central Havana. The plaza dates way back to the 16th century, so there are plenty of old beautiful buildings around the square, and plenty of cafes offering a strong cappuccino so that you can take in the view while enjoying a coffee.

69. Explore the Magical Bellamar Caves

The Bellamar Caves is one of the leading tourist attractions in Cuba, and it's with good reason. The only way of exploring the caves is with a tour, but it's well worth the splurge. First of all, you will descend into a great cavern where you will see incredible stalactite and stalagmite formations. You will then wind through narrower caverns, and you will even be able to see crystal formations, and drink from the perfectly clear waters.

(Carretera A Las Cuevas, Matanzas)

70. Cool Down With an Ice Cream From Coppelia

Cuba can be staggeringly hot at virtually any time of the year, and what better way is there to cool down with a creamy ice cream? We can guarantee that you'll taste some of the best ice cream of your life in Cuba, specifically if you visit the Cuban institution called Coppelia in Havana. This place was opened by the state in 1966 and has been astoundingly popular ever since. Since you can pay in the local currency, the ice cream is very cheap, and the sharing tables offer the perfect opportunity to make local friends.

71. Swim in the Pool Below Salto de Soroa

There is nothing quite as beautiful as a cascading waterfall that you stumble upon in the wilderness. If you are a waterfall junkie, you absolutely need to know about the Salto de Sorao in Sorao. The waterfall is just north of the orchid garden, and you can take a short hike there yourself. Once there, it is perfectly safe to cool off by taking a dip in the pool at the bottom of the waterfall. What better way of enjoying a warm day in Cuba?

72. Have an Artsy Day at the Museo Nacional de Bellas Artes

Because of Cuba's distance from the rest of the world, you'd be totally forgiven for not having much of a clue about Cuban art, but the truth is that the island country has had a vibrant arts culture, and this is best discovered at the Museum Nacional de Bellas Artes in Havana. One of the two buildings of the museum is completely dedicated to Cuban artworks from the 17th-19th centuries, including landscapes, religious paintings, and artworks dedicated to portraying social life in Cuba.

(www.bellasartes.cult.cu)

73. Have a Sky Diving Adventure at Centro Internacional de Paracadismo

As the largest beach resort in all of the Caribbean, Varadero is a veritable beach paradise for sun worshippers. But when you want to do something a little bit more adventurous than another day paddling in the ocean, what is there to do? Well, it's possible to have a sky diving adventure over the beach with the aid of Internacional de Paracadismo. You'll jump from a 3000 metre height, and you'll experience a 35 second freefall – thrilling!

(www.skydivingvaradero.com)

74. Sip on Mojitos in Havana's Most Famous Bar

If you love nothing more than hopping from bar to bar, Havana is a city that will be right up your street because it has an incredibly vibrant bar culture. Perhaps the most famous bar in the whole city, and that you need to visit at least once, is La Bodeguita del Medio. This bar is famous because of its many famous customers, such as Pablo Neruda and Salvador Allende, and because it claims to be the birthplace of the mojito. And, of course, when you visit, a mojito is exactly what you need to order.

(Empedrado, La Habana; www.labodeguita.com)

75. Enjoy the Green Oasis of Parque Josone

Varadero is best known for its stunning beaches, but if you have the need for the green, there are also some spots where you can get back to nature, and we particularly love the Parque Josone. You can find these beautifully landscaped gardens, which date back to the 1940s, a little way inland from the coast. There are atmospheric eateries in the open air inside the park, a lake so that you can enjoy some romantic boating, and you can often find locals celebrating their birthdays inside the park too.

(Avenida 4ta, Varadero)

76. Visit the Original Bacardi Rum Factory

Bacardi, the famous rum brand that is enjoyed all over the world, is nothing short of a Cuban institution. If you have the time, it can be a wonderful idea to visit the original Bacardi factory in Santiago to get to grips with the brand's history and legacy. The factory opened in the 19th century, and while Bacardi jumped ship from Cuba after the Revolution, rum is still produced in the factory. In fact, nine million litres of rum are produced in the factory each and every year.

(Narciso Lopez, Santiago de Cuba)

77. Relax in Havana's Oldest Square, Plaza de Armas

Plazas are an important part of Latin American culture, and this is certainly true of Cuba. The oldest square in Havana is called Plaza de Armas, it was constructed way back in 1520, and it's well worth a visit. There are gardens around the square, which make it a pleasant place to hang out on a sunny day, and there is also a daily secondhand book market in the square, which can be a great place to visit if you want to brush up your Spanish skills.

78. Get Back to Nature at the Cienfuegos Botanical Gardens

Okay, so these botanical gardens actually lie around 25km outside of Cienfuegos, but if you are a nature lover, it's certainly worth making the trip, because these are often considered to be the best botanical gardens in the country. The gardens were founded in 1899 by a

New England botanist, and today the gardens host around 1490 plant species, including 89 rubber trees and 400 cactus species. It's well worth taking the guided tour if you want to learn more about the plant life inside the gardens.

(Km 15, Circuito Sur, Pepito Tey)

79. Spend an Evening at an Upscale Piano Bar

While the sounds of salsa and rumba music around Havana can be intoxicating, you might have nights when you want something a little less frenetic, and when that moment comes, we can recommend an evening spent at the Bar-Club Imagenes. This piano bar is the place for dim lighting and to listen to slow piano ballads while tucking into one of the bar's very affordable meals.

(Calzada #602)

80. Climb the Tower of Catedral de San Cristobal

If you are a fan of religious architecture, there are plenty of treasures for you to explore in Cuba, and particularly in Havana. The most spectacular religious building of them all in Havana has to be the Catedral de San Cristobal. The intricate baroque façade was described by the author Alejo Carpentier as "music set in stone". What's more, it's actually possible to go inside and climb the tower of the cathedral to get a great view over the city.

(Empedrado, La Habana)

81. Discover Coastal Village Life in Maria La Gorda

When you want to have an incredible beach break, but you'd rather avoid the touristy spots with all inclusive hotels, where are you supposed to go in Cuba? One of our favourite coastal villages is Maria la Gorda, precisely for the reason that it is really remote and that gives you the chance to experience authentic coastal village life in Cuba, and to completely relax and unwind without all night beach parties.

82. Enjoy Seafood With a View at Finca Del Mar

As an island, you might expect Cuba to have more of a variety of seafood than it has. While it's true that the local population doesn't veer too far away from rice and beans, you can certainly track down some great seafood if you put your mind to it, and we really love the food at Finca Del Mar in Cienfuegos. This restaurant is situated in the harbour so you get to experience a killer view and great seafood at the same time. If you don't mind splurging, we can heartily recommend the lobster.

(Calle 35, Cienfuegos)

83. Buy Beautiful Perfume at Habana 1971

While we're pretty sure that nobody travels to Cuba just to buy perfume, if you are somebody who is crazy for scents, you cannot leave without visiting the perfume shop called Habana 1971. This shop is located in a stunning 18th century mansion in the heart of Old Havana, but you will smell the shop long before you see it. They have 12 scents that have been rescued from colonial Cuba, and all the perfumes in the store are totally handcrafted. These make for exceptional gifts. *(156 Mercaderes, La Habana)*

84. Rent a Luxury Car From Rex

As you walk around the streets of Cuba, something that is bound to catch your eye is the quality of the incredible cars that line the streets. If you fancy getting behind the wheel and experiencing some of this automobile luxury for yourself, this is totally possible, you just have to visit a car rental shop called Rex, which has shops all around the country. They offer the standard rental cars, but also many luxury options so you can drive around just like a real Cuban.

(www.rex.cu)

85. Watch a Classical Music Show at Teatro Amadeo Roldan

The Teatro Amadeo Roldan, built in 1929, is one of the most important theatres in Havana. Unfortunately, it was destroyed by a pyromaniac in 1977, but reopened its doors in 1999 when it became the head office for the National Symphony Orchestra of Cuba. Of course, this means that this theatre is the most important performance venue for classical music in the whole country, and if you want to take in a classical music show, this is the place for you.

86. Get Back to Nature in Parque Natural Majayara

If you find yourself in Baracoa, and you want to explore some of the beautiful nature nearby, you should absolutely spend a day at the Parque Natural Majayara, which is by no means one of the largest parks in the country, but it is packed with beauty and charm. There is an archaeological hike within the park, as well as a couple of other hiking opportunities, and even natural pools that you can swim in after a picnic lunch in nature – perfect!

87. Celebrate Cuban Culture With Fiesta de la Cubania

Predating Havana, Bayamo is one of the most important cities in all of Cuba, and yet it often goes unvisited by tourists. If you fancy a trip to this city, any time of the year is good, but it really comes to life during La Fiesta de la Cubania, a festival that simply celebrates everything Cuban, and which is hosted in the city every October. Of course, you can expect rumba music, salsa music, trovas, plenty of dancing, and more than just a little bit of rum swilling as well.

88. Be Wowed by Beautiful Morro Castle

As you walk around the perfectly picturesque streets of Havana, you are likely to spot something on the coastal horizon, and that would be a fortress called Morro. The fortress was designed by an Italian in the 16th century, and on the site of the castle today you can spot a moat, a lighthouse, a museum of the lighthouses around Cuba, an underwater archaeological exhibition, and dungeons, guns, and batteries.

89. Try a Plate of Swedish-Cuban Fusion Food

When you think of two cultures that are about as far removed from each other as is humanly possible, you might think of Sweden and Cuba. And so it is no small thing that there is a Swedish-Cuban restaurant in Havana called Casa Miglis. But what exactly is Swedish-Cuban food, you might be wondering. Well, on the menu of Casa Miglis you can find meatballs and mashed potatoes, ceviche, and beef chilli with lingonberries. And it's all pretty tasty.

(Lealtad, La Habana; www.casamiglis.com)

90. Catch a Performance at the International Ballet Festival in Havana

When you think of the places in the world most famous for stunning ballet performances, Cuba is probably not the first country that would spring to mind. But that is not to say that there is not a ballet culture here, and if you do love a ballet show, you will be mesmerised during the International Ballet Festival in Havana, which is hosted every two years in the

Grand Theatre of Havana. Ballet companies from all over the world are invited to perform, and it's one of the most important festivals on the Cuban cultural calendar.

91. Get to Grips With the Colonial Architecture of Trinidad

As you walk around the charming town of Trinidad, you would be forgiven for thinking that you have been trapped in the 18th century. Much of the colonial architecture has been preserved from this period, and if you would like to learn more about it, the Museum of Colonial Architecture is well worth a visit. Inside, there are many displays of architectural trimmings such as doors, handles, windows, grates, and locks, and the guided tours are 100% worth the money.

(Calle Desengaño #83, Trinidad)

92. Hike the Mountains of Vinales National Park

For nature lovers visiting Cuba, there is one place that stands head and shoulders above everywhere else in the country, and that's the Vinales National Park. In fact, this park is so alluring that it's Cuba's second most visited destination after Havana. There are countless hiking trails here, and you'll be walking through real farmland so you'll get to see some of the real Cuba. You'll also have the opportunity to hike up mountains, through caves, and to incredible viewpoints. Strap on those hiking boots.

93. Watch a Charlie Chaplin Movie at Café Arcangel

When you've done just about as much sightseeing as you can possibly muster and you're looking for a place in Havana to relax and unwind, we reckon that Café Arcangel is just the place. They serve up really fantastic coffee, light as air cakes, there is soft music, but the thing we love most of all is that they will often project silent Charlie Chaplin movies on to the wall. What's cooler than that?

(57 Concordia, La Habana; www.cafearcangel.com/index.html)

94. Take in a View of Holguin from Loma de la Cruz

One of the most famous and celebrated in Cuba is La Loma de la Cruz, which is essentially a huge cross that was raised in 1790 with the hopes of it combatting a devastating drought. To get to the Loma de la Cruz, you will need some strong legs as it's a 465 step hike up a hill to get there. The rewards of the view of the surrounding Holguin area are, however, more than worth it, so make sure you get a good night of sleep the night before.

95. Find Something Special to Take Home at Guardalavaca

If you are struggling with souvenir shopping in Cuba because you would prefer to avoid the obvious things like bottles of rum and Cuban cigars, you might be interested in visiting a quaint beach town in the Holguin region of Cuba called Guardalavaca. The beach is lovely here, by the way, but if you're on a shopping expedition, you'll be interested in the Guardalavaca flea market, a cute market where you can find artisanal items and antiques.

96. Indulge an Inner Chocaholic at Museo de Chocolate

Who doesn't love chocolate, right? Well, Cuba is a country that produces some of the finest chocolate in the whole world and a trip to Cuba would not be complete without visiting the Museo de Chocolate for any chocolate lover. But if you are thinking that you'd rather taste the stuff than learn about it, fear not because this is very much a café with a museum as a side gig. You can choose dark, white, hot, cold, rich, smooth – however you want it.

(Calle Amargura, La Habana)

97. Visit an Indigenous Cemetery, Chorro de Maita

You might think that Cuban culture is all salsa and rum, but actually there is an indigenous culture in Cuba that is very unexplored. If you would like to get to grips with this part of Cuba, we can recommend a trip to Chorro de Maita, an archaeological site based museum that is centred around an Indian village and cemetery. You can see the remains of over 60 very well preserved human skeletons, and there are also some recreations of Indian village life back in the 16th century.

98. Take a Relaxing Harbour Boat Trip Around Cienfuegos

Cienfuegos, otherwise known as the Pearl of the South, is a city that is all too often overlooked by tourists visiting Cuba. This small port city was actually founded by the French, and so it has a very different feel to other places in the country. One of the nicest things to do there is take a boat trip around the bay. If you are really lucky, you will even be able to see dolphins jumping in the waters.

99. Rock Out at the National Rock Atenas Festival

When you think of places to go to for a bangin'
summer festival experience, Cuba is probably not the
first place that you think of. But if you can drag
yourself away from Burning Man, you might just find
that the National Rock Atenas Festival, which is hosted
in Varadero every year in early June, could be up your
alley. This is one of the largest rock events in the
country, so if you feel like a break from the salsa music
from a moment, why not try this festival out for size?

100. Try Your Hand at Rock Climbing in Vinales

For outdoorsy types, Cuba is an incredible destination,
particularly if you make it to the Vinales National Park,
where rock climbing is one of the most popular
activities for adventurers. And don 't fear if you are a
climbing virgin because there are numerous tour
companies in the region that would love to show you
the ropes and can provide you with all the climbing
gear you need to have an epic climb in the Cuban
countryside that you will never forget.

101. Eat Yummy Coconut Pie From the Street

With its tropical climate, there is no shortage of coconuts in Cuba, and this means that you can find an array of coconut flavoured desserts and drinks all over the country. One of our favourite coconut flavoured treats is the humble coconut pie, which can be found all over the streets of Cuba. It's essentially shredded coconut baked into a shortcrust pastry crust, and to be honest, it couldn't be any better.

Before You Go...

Thanks for reading **101 Coolest Things to Do in Cuba.** We hope that it makes your trip a memorable one!

Keep your eyes peeled on www.101coolestthings.com, and have a wonderful time in Cuba.

Team 101 Coolest Things

Printed in Great Britain
by Amazon